Shrine of St. Alban — Early 14th century

ROYAL COMMISSION ON HISTORICAL MONUMENTS (ENGLAND)

A GUIDE TO SAINT ALBANS CATHEDRAL

LONDON
HER MAJESTY'S STATIONERY OFFICE

First published 1952
Second edition 1982
Second impression 1989

ISBN 0 11 701128 2

Cover. South elevation in 1875, part of a drawing from J. E. Neale's, *The Abbey Church of St. Alban, Herts.*, [1878].

Preface

This account of the Abbey church, now the Cathedral, of St. Albans is founded in the main on the survey of that great building undertaken by the Royal Commission on Historical Monuments (England) and published in the *Inventory of the Historical Monuments in Hertfordshire*, 1910. This first volume issued by the Commission has long been out of print and the opportunity has been taken to make a thorough revision of the account originally given; at the same time the history of the building has been discussed at greater length than is customary in the Commission's Inventories and the description cast in a form which it is hoped will make for easier reading without any grave sacrifice of accuracy or completeness.

The Royal Commission on Historical Monuments must first acknowledge its debt to the Victoria County History of Hertfordshire whose account of St. Albans Abbey, published in 1902, was the forerunner and foundation of its own. The Commissioners wish to thank the Dean and Chapter of St. Albans and the Surveyor to the fabric for their kindness and assistance.

Note on this revised edition: the text has been amended in places, though the form of the original *Guide* has been retained. The opportunity has been taken to include a summary and illustrations of the results of the 1978 excavations on the site of the mediaeval chapter house; its successor is under construction at the time of writing. We would again thank the Dean and Chapter for their assistance.

1981

ACKNOWLEDGEMENTS

For the use of illustrations in this Guide the Commission is indebted to the following: Aerofilms Ltd., for the air photograph on Plate 1; the Reverend Canon M. H. Ridgway, for photographs taken by the late Mr. F. H. Crossley and comprising the detail of the Lady chapel on Plate 7, the view of the north side of the nave on Plate 8, of the nave piers on Plate 10 and of the triforium of the south transept on Plate 12; Professor Martin Biddle and Mrs. Birthe Kjølbye-Biddle, for plans, adapted by the Commission, on Plate 14.

BIBLIOGRAPHY

Amundesham-Annales Mon. S. Albani, Riley, H. T., ed., Rolls Series 28, 1870/71).

Beckett, Sir Edward, Lord Grimthorpe, *St. Albans Cathedral and its Restoration . . .*, St. Albans 1885, 2nd ed. 1890.

Biddle M. and Kjølbye-Biddle B., 'The Medieval Chapter House of St. Albans Abbey, and its Excavation in 1978', *Expedition* (The University Museum Magazine of Archaeology/Anthropology, University of Pennsylvania) 22, no. 2, 1980.

Buckler, I. C. and C. A., *A History of the Abbey Church of St. Alban*, London 1847.

Gesta Abbatum Mon. S. Albani, Riley, H. T., ed., Rolls Series 28, 1867/9.

Lowe, W. R. L. et al, eds., *Illustrations of the Life of St. Alban*, Oxford 1924.

Micklethwaite, J. T., 'The Shrine of St. Alban', *Archaeological Journal*, 29, 1872.

Neale, James, *The Abbey Church of St. Alban, Herts.*, London, [1878].

North, J. D., *Richard of Wallingford*, Oxford 1976.

Page, William, 'Paintings in the Nave of St. Albans Cathedral', *Archaeologia* 58, 1902.

Registrum Abbatis Johannis Whethamstede, Riley, H. T. ed., Rolls Series 28, 1872/3.

Royal Commission on Historical Monuments (England): *Hertfordshire*, 1910.

The Victoria History of the Counties of England: *Hertfordshire* 2, 1908 and 4, 1914.

Contents

List of Illustrations

SAINT ALBANS CATHEDRAL

HISTORICAL INTRODUCTION

The Cathedral, formerly the Abbey Church, of St. Albans stands on the slope of a low hill on the south-west side of the mediaeval town, above the river Ver and almost opposite the site of Roman Verulamium. It is said to be on the spot where St. Alban was martyred. Alban was a Roman of Verulamium who according to legend gave shelter to, and was converted by, Amphibalus, a Christian fleeing from pagan persecution. Charged with these crimes, and refusing to deny his new faith, Alban was led out of the city to execution. The river Ver dried up to allow the accompanying multitude to pass over, a spring burst out of the hillside to quench the martyr's last thirst and, as the executioner brought down his sword, his eyes dropped out of his head. The story goes back to a 'passio' of the saints composed early in the sixth century and elaborated in the usual manner of such records, but the localisation of the cult outside the Roman city of Verulamium is attested both by the accuracy of the topographical detail and by a continuous tradition. The most likely date for the martyrdom is the year 209 when the Emperor Severus and his sons Caracalla and Gaeta were in Britain.

Bede, writing in the early eighth century, records the continued existence of a beautiful church built on the site of the martyrdom and adds that it was the scene of frequent cures. At the end of the same century gifts of land by Offa, King of Mercia, and his son Egfrith bear witness to the existence of a wealthy monastery here. The Abbey shared in the monastic reform movement of the late tenth century in the time of Abbot Aelfric and by 1086, although not the wealthiest of English abbeys, it had a comfortable income of £270 a year. In the course of the twelfth century the abbot obtained the right to wear the mitre and the recognition of the Abbey's independence of the bishop of Lincoln; Pope Adrian IV, who granted this, was a native of Abbots Langley, a manor belonging to the Abbey. At the Council of Tours in 1163, St. Albans claimed to be the first among English abbeys; such pretensions did not go undisputed, but certainly its reputation was very high in the twelfth and thirteenth centuries. On several occasions monks of St Albans were called upon to rule other abbeys and among its daughter houses were such considerable institutions as Tynemouth in the North and Wymondham and Binham Priories in Norfolk. The twelfth and thirteenth centuries were a great period for art and literature at the Abbey. The St. Albans Psalter, *c.*1130, opened a new phase in the history of English painting: Roger of Wendover (d.1236) was the first in an important line of St. Albans chroniclers; Matthew Paris (d.1259), historian and painter, was also a man of affairs and was invited to Norway by King Haakon IV to reform the Abbey of St. Benet Holm. The great fame of the Abbey brought it many gifts of land and the *Taxatio Ecclesiastica* of 1291 reckoned its income at £850 a year: this is probably a conservative estimate. From the fourteenth century onwards it lived mainly on its past reputation and the reputations of such notable abbots as Richard of Wallingford and John of Wheathampstead, though in the abbacy of Thomas Delamare, 1349–96, it occupied a position in the country almost comparable to that of its great age a century before. By the end of the fifteenth century St. Albans was a great and ancient institution and nothing more, and its suppression in 1539 was affected as quietly and easily as was that of most of its sister abbeys. The church was used partly as a parish council and partly as a grammar school for the next three hundred years. By the late nineteenth century the need to re-organise the diocesan system and create new sees had long been apparent and the first bishop of St. Albans was enthroned in 1877, but it was not until 1900 that the Chapter was constituted as a corporate body.

ARCHITECTURAL HISTORY

The history of the existing building, up to the Reformation, has four distinct phases: the construction of the main body of the present church from 1077 to about 1115; the extensions to the west end between 1195 and 1235; the remodelling and extension of the east end from 1256 to the beginning of the fourteenth century; and minor alterations to the fabric and the major furnishings of the interior in the late fourteenth, the fifteenth and the early sixteenth centuries.

The rebuilding by Abbot Paul of Caen begun in 1077 was in line with the general development in England immediately after the Conquest. In nearly every case as soon as the first Norman abbot was sure of his position he began to rebuild. This may have been partly arrogance and ill-founded contempt for the native architecture—Paul called his predecessors at St. Albans 'rudes et idiotas'—partly 'prestige building' to glorify the new regime, and partly, of course, the expression in England of that great church-building movement of a developing and confident feudal society that covered Western Europe in the eleventh century with 'a white robe of churches'. In any event the church would probably have been rebuilt about this time, for the Saxon abbots had been collecting materials from Verulamium for the purpose since the beginning of the century. Paul made great use of this material and the Norman church was built almost wholly of Roman brick. Those parts of Paul's building which still stand are the two westernmost bays of the presbytery with their north and south aisles, the central tower except for the battlements, the transepts, of which the north and south walls have been rebuilt above the ground storey, the nine easternmost bays of the north arcade of the nave and the three easternmost bays of the south arcade with the corresponding parts of their aisles. The rest of the eleventh-century church has been destroyed but its plan is reasonably certain. The Norman nave was of ten bays and the presbytery extended eastwards to the west end of the present ambulatory and terminated in an apse that was probably semi-circular externally. Its aisles extended almost to the east end of the existing aisles and terminated in apses which were probably square externally and whose exterior walls were on the line of the present east end of the presbytery and its aisles. There were also two contiguous apsidal chapels on the east side of each transept, the chapel against the presbytery aisle wall extending farther east than its neighbour. The solid walls between presbytery and aisles relate Paul's church to an extensive group of eleventh-century churches in North West Europe which had, or were intended to have, barrel vaults over their eastern arms. The walls provided the necessary support for such vaults, and in this respect the immediate precedents for St. Albans were Lanfranc's church at Canterbury and the abbey of La Trinité at Caen. However, St. Albans was longer and wider than any of these and there was room for two chapels on each transept arm. The inner chapel on each arm projected farther than the outer and the two linked up in echelon with the chapels and the main apse of the choir. A precursor and possible model was the great Cluniac priory at La Charité-sur-Loire. Paul appears to have been well satisfied with the work done, for he made a grant of lands at Syreth and Wantone and of a house in St. Albans to 'Robert the Mason', who is described as superior to all other masons of his time. From an entry in the *Gesta Abbatum*—a chronicle of the Abbey—it is possible that the church was completed or nearing completion at the time of Anselm's enthronement as Archbishop of Canterbury in 1093. It was not dedicated, however, until 1115, and knowing how later building ventures at St. Albans dawdled for lack of funds we may infer that Paul's church was not, in fact, completed until well into the twelfth century.

For nearly a century after the completion of the Norman church the monastic buildings were the abbot's main care. In 1195 John de Cella succeeded to the abbacy and decided to extend the nave three bays westward and build a new west front. From the architectural remains it is clear that the new front was intended to have flanking north and south towers and projecting vaulted porches. Difficulties were soon encountered and the flanking towers were never built. Work was stopped completely in 1197 and from 1199 went on very slowly until John's death in 1214. William of Trumpington succeeded him and by a more energetic policy had completed the western extension at his death in 1235. The insertion of a great west window by John of Wheathampstead in the fifteenth century and the more recent restoration by Lord Grimthorpe have left little of the new front. It is possible, however, that the richly ornamented arcading hidden behind Grimthorpe's work in the north porch is by John. The comparison of this with the presumed later work seems to show that William was forced to economise on his predecessor's plans in order to complete them. The preparations for vaulting shafts show that it was originally intended to vault the new bays in stone but this too had to be abandoned and a cheaper wooden roof substituted. That money difficulties were the cause of William's economy seems clear, for the Abbey suffered severely in the troubles of John's reign. Its losses in this period were estimated at £2,555, then a huge sum of money. It seems to have been regarded as an extraordinary source of income by John and as an easy source of plunder by any army that happened to be in the neighbourhood. It is a tribute to William's resource that besides the other work he rebuilt the three easternmost bays of the south aisle of the presbytery, rebuilt in stone many of the brick windows of Paul of Caen and erected a lead-covered wooden spire over the central crossing. His death in 1235 marks the end of the second phase of the Abbey's architectural history and his rebuilding of the south aisle of the presbytery foreshadows the character of the third phase.

By the middle of the thirteenth century St. Alban and his Abbey were at the height of their fame. It is therefore not surprising that the monks decided that their Saint deserved a better home for his shrine than the existing presbytery and their church a finer east end than the old-fashioned one it had. The appearance of dangerous cracks in the presbytery walls in 1257 made the matter urgent and the rebuilding was begun. The two westernmost bays of the north aisle and the three westernmost bays of the south aisle were left in position, probably because the solid presbytery walls were regarded as buttresses which would take the great weight of the central tower and of the spire upon it. The rest of the presbytery, with its aisles, was pulled down and rebuilt, and the ambulatory, ante-chapel, and Lady chapel erected. The completion of what was essentially a single piece of building took over fifty years, and alterations in the plan and changes in design and decoration were made as the building progressed eastwards. Again achievement fell short of desire and the intended stone vault of the presbytery, the vault and central columns of the ambulatory and the stone vault of the Lady chapel had to be abandoned. The wooden vault of the presbytery is the earliest surviving example of its kind on a large scale. The flowing and geometrical character of the tracery of the windows of the Lady chapel, in combination with the enriched decoration around the jambs internally, is of a very advanced design for the date, *c.* 1308, usually assigned to it. It is doubtful, however, if the documentary evidence can be made to support this early date and the windows may be considerably later.

With the completion of the Lady chapel the fabric of the church was, in general, much as we see it today. From then until the Reformation the work carried out was mainly necessary repairs and minor alterations to the structure and the provision of screens and chantry chapels. The one major repair was to five bays on the south side of the nave, the fourth to the eighth from the east, which fell in 1323. The work of repair was immediately begun by Abbot Hugh of Eversden but it was not completed until the abbacy of Michael of Mentmore (1335–49). The delay was due to the attitude of Eversden's successor, Richard of Wallingford, intellectually perhaps the greatest of all abbots. He devoted much of his time to perfecting his astronomical clock, and, when reproved by the King for neglecting the repairs, remarked, with some justice, that many of his successors would be able to get a church repaired but none of them would be able to complete his clock. John of Wheathampstead, in his first abbacy (1420–40), inserted a great window in the west front and built the chapel of the Transfiguration at the south-east corner of the Lady chapel, and a chapel, now destroyed, south of the first bay from the east of the south aisle of the presbytery. Later in the fifteenth century William of Wallingford inserted great windows in the north and south transepts. Between 1454–62 the parishioners' chapel of St. Andrew was again rebuilt.

At some time in the same century or possibly early in the sixteenth century the spire that William of Trumpington had erected was taken down and a very low spire, of local type and known as a 'Hertfordshire Spike', was put in its place. Apart from this, the main work of the period from the late fourteenth to the middle of the sixteenth century was the provision of furnishings and internal decorations of the church: the chapel of Humphrey of Gloucester, the so-called 'Chapel of Wheathampstead', the tomb and chapel of Abbot Ramryge, the reredos and the rood screen, the brasses, of which that of Abbot Delamare is outstanding, and the redecoration of the wooden roofs, the last carried out mainly by Wheathampstead.

With the Dissolution of the Abbey in 1539 begins the most melancholy period of its architectural history. The monastic buildings were sold to an official of the Royal Works, Sir Richard Lee, for building materials. The church was sold to the town of St. Albans and the chapel of St. Andrew pulled down. The arches at the east end of the presbytery were walled up and a public passageway made through the west bay of the ambulatory. The other bays and the Lady chapel were turned into a grammar school. From time to time repairs were carried out. When James I visited St. Albans in 1612 a sum of £2,000 was raised and between 1721 and 1724, when Nicholas Hawksmoor was called in to advise, several thousand pounds were spent. Nevertheless, as an early eighteenth-century historian of Hertfordshire sadly remarked, 'This noble Fabrick hath, since it became a Parish Church, wanted its Abbots Zeal and Purse too for repairs'. The epoch of 'laisser tomber' had begun. It bore fruit in 1832 when a part of the wall below a clearstorey window on the south side of the nave fell through the roof of the south aisle. Repairs were carried out by the architect L. N. Cottingham and on his advice the 'Hertfordshire Spike' was removed to lessen the weight on the tower. From then on, with the increasing interest in mediaeval architecture and the increasing danger of the fall of the whole building, greater efforts were made at repair and restoration. From 1856 to 1877 Sir Gilbert Scott was in charge of the works. He partly restored the ten western clearstorey windows on the south of the nave, re-roofed part of the south aisle, restored the exterior stonework of the Lady chapel and saved the central tower from falling and rendered it safe. The passageway through the ambulatory was shut and the Lady chapel reunited with the rest of the church. After Scott's death Sir Edmund Beckett, later Lord Grimthorpe, obtained a faculty in 1880 giving him complete control over the restoration. His work may be seen nearly everywhere but its main features are the west front, which he almost entirely rebuilt, the north and south ends of the transepts, the internal restoration of the Lady chapel and ambulatory and the restoration, or rather the saving, of the nave. He spent nearly a quarter of a million pounds on the task and one cannot deny that there is something to show for the money. He aroused great opposition and criticism but nobody else at the time was ready to undertake the heavy financial responsibility and it is due to Grimthorpe that there is today a cathedral at St. Albans and not a heap of ruins.

ARCHITECTURAL DESCRIPTION

THE LADY CHAPEL (Plates 2 and 7)

The Lady chapel, completed early in the fourteenth century, is remarkable for the developed character of the tracery of its windows and for the richness and elaboration of the ornament on their internal splays. There is some documentary evidence that suggests a date just after 1308 for the completion of the chapel, but the evidence is equivocal and the second window on the south must certainly be subsequent to this, for it is of a type that appears much later in the century. Much of the external stonework is modern but internally the tracery and mullions are mainly old. The figures in the window niches are generally too damaged for identification. In the middle window on the north the top figure on the east jamb is Edward the Confessor and, opposite, on the west jamb, St. Edmund. In the middle window on the south the bottom figure on the central mullion is probably St. Stephen, and in the west window the top figures on the central mullion are Our Lady with St. Anne. On the west jamb of the same window are the remains of a decorative scheme—floral decoration on a red background, and a portion of a text—probably that carried out by Wheathampstead between 1420 and 1440.

In the south-east bay is a curved triangular window above the canopied sedilia and piscina. The square-headed opening in the back of the eastern sedile, now blocked, led through into the chapel of the Transfiguration. The present chapel of the Transfiguration, completely rebuilt by Lord Grimthorpe, is on the site of the chapel built by William Brydone, one of the monks, and consecrated in 1430. This chapel is shown in seventeenth and eighteenth-century engravings with a high-pitched roof that must have blocked the triangular window in the Lady chapel. By the early nineteenth century a flat roof had been substituted and the chapel was being used as a library. Under the ceiling are four re-set corbels which may have carried the original roof. The door into the Lady chapel is modern.

It had been intended to vault the Lady chapel in stone but the idea was abandoned and a wooden vault substituted. Lord Grimthorpe replaced this with the present stone vault. The arcading below the windows is a modern restoration carried out under Lord Grimthorpe by a local carver. The capitals of the shafts are enriched with realistic renderings of common wild flowers. The original arcading had cinquefoiled heads on the south and trefoiled heads on the north, and was much like that in the south aisle of the ambulatory.

THE AMBULATORY

The ambulatory, part of which occupies the site of the destroyed central apse of Paul of Caen, is intermediate in date between the presbytery and the Lady chapel and has characteristics of both. Its history is difficult to disentangle. The first portions begun were probably the south and east walls of the south aisle, for they seem to have carried on the design of the two east bays of the south aisle of the presbytery. The wall arcade in the west bay of the north aisle carries on the design of that in the north aisle of the presbytery, but the east window of the north aisle, although of late thirteenth-century type, has tracery similar to that in the Lady chapel and was probably the last part of the ambulatory to be completed. The design of the wall arcading of the south aisle is continued into the Lady chapel and is perhaps nearly contemporary with it.

It was originally intended to vault the central space in three equal spans with high-pitched stone vaults, and the sleeper walls to carry the central piers have been found beneath the present floors. Before Lord Grimthorpe's restoration the springers intended for this vaulting were to be seen, and the blank space left by their cutting away can still be seen on the easternmost pier of the north arcade. The design was never carried through, presumably because of the cost, and a flat wooden ceiling was put up instead, decorated, under Abbot Hugh of Eversden, with a painting of the Assumption. The present ceilings are all modern restorations by Scott and Grimthorpe.

At the east end of the south aisle stood the altar of the Four Tapers; near its steps was a door leading into the monks' cemetery, to the east of the south transept. The blocked door at the north end of the east wall led originally into a staircase to the roof of the Lady chapel. In the south wall of the east bay are three recesses with two piscina drains, presumably for the use of this altar and apparently contemporary with the aisle.

In the central space stood the shrine of St. Amphibalus. The restored pedestal of the shrine is now in the north aisle of the presbytery.

After the Dissolution the west bay was converted into a public footpath through the church and a wall was built across its eastern end, shutting off the school in the Lady chapel. A steeply gabled porch was built at the north end of the passage and at the south the tracery of the window above was removed and the opening partly filled with brick in a unique design of a circular light above two rectangular ones.

THE PRESBYTERY

The original Norman presbytery, of which the western part still remains, was probably the same length as the present one. The first alterations were probably those of William of Trumpington in the south aisle where he appears to have rebuilt the three easternmost bays with groined vaults of a slightly higher pitch than in the westernmost bays. At the rebuilding of 1257 and later, when Roman brick was used on a considerable scale for the last time, the two easternmost bays of the presbytery and south aisle and the three easternmost bays of the north aisle were taken down and rebuilt and the fourth bay from the east of the north aisle was revaulted. This meant that two of the three bays rebuilt by William were pulled down and the existence of springers on the western piers of the third bay from the east seems to suggest that it was originally intended to pull down the next bay as well. The old walls to the west which were left standing were thinned back on the inside to range with the new walls to the east. The original entries into the presbytery from the aisles at the west were partly blocked and new entrances made and provided with richly decorated canopy work. These tabernacles were later broken up and built into the walls. That now to be seen on the south was found in pieces in 1850 and re-erected; that on the north is a modern copy dating from Lord Grimthorpe's restoration. The original clearstorey was probably very similar to the existing Norman clearstorey in the nave. It was replaced in this rebuilding by the present one of five windows on each side, each with three lights, with plain lancets and pierced spandrels. The tracery now in the clearstorey windows is modern and does not reproduce the original design.

The plainness of the original tracery was probably due to the same need for economy that prevented the erection of a stone vault. The remains of vaulting shafts internally and of abutments for flying buttresses on the exterior are clear proof that a stone vault was intended. Instead, the existing wooden vault was erected. Such wooden vaults were never very common in the greater churches and, since the fires at Selby and York, that at St. Albans is probably the earliest of any importance still in existence. When the roof was repaired in 1930, carpenters' marks were found on the timbers and it is probable that the roof was first erected on the ground and then dismantled and placed in position. Its original decorations were obliterated by John of Wheathampstead, who is responsible for the present design of circular medallions enclosing the Eagle and the Lamb, the symbols of John the Evangelist and John the Baptist. Wheathampstead appears also to have altered the ribbing of the vault and to have substituted the present surface ribs, running from the springers to the transverse ribs, for the original lierne ribs whose traces can still be seen under Wheathampstead's decorations. A consequence of this alteration was a moving of the bosses, originally at the junctions of the lierne ribs with the transverse ribs, down to the new rib junctions. The roof was repaired in 1680–1 when new backbones were given to the lower ends of some of the ribs. The present shields which mask the junction of the stone springers and the wooden ribs date from this repair and commemorate those who contributed to it (Plate 11). The roof was found to be very worm-eaten in 1930, when it was repaired and made safe with a steel backbone.

At the north end of the east wall of the presbytery is a painting of a figure in archbishop's vestments and probably meant for St. William, Archbishop of York from 1140–54. The arms shown, *lozengy argent and gules*, are the arms known to have been borne by the Fitzwilliam family in the fourteenth century. The painting is of late fourteenth-century date. At the south end is a band of floral patterning, probably of the same date.

The *North Aisle* of the presbytery retains in its westernmost bay a groined eleventh-century vault. The wall arcading with the stone bench under the windows is of the late thirteenth century and its design is continued into the ambulatory. The arch under the recess in the first bay from the east was found elsewhere and placed here by Sir Gilbert Scott. The carving in its spandrels is nineteenth-century work. In the fourth bay from the west a fifteenth-century doorway has been inserted, cutting across the arcading and partly obliterating the shafts in the window jambs. The window in the north wall at the west end is modern. Until the destruction of the apsidal chapels of the north transept there was no room for a window here.

The *South Aisle* has undergone much alteration and contains work of many periods. At the west end it retains two eleventh-century bays with their groined vaulting. The round-headed brick arch in the south wall of the westernmost bay must have led into the apsidal chapel of the south transept. The round-headed opening above it may have been intended to obtain light for this dark part of the aisle from the upper part of the chapel. The unusual double opening in the south wall of the second bay from the west was for the same purpose and was probably, at this height, beyond the westward termination of the apsidal chapel. When the chapel was pulled down a vestry with a treasury above was built in its place at some time in the fourteenth century. This building was not apsidal and, at the level of this double opening, probably projected farther eastwards than the chapel had done. The later window, cutting into the original double opening on the east, was therefore presumably made in order to get light from beyond the eastward termination of the new building. The third bay from the west is the only one remaining of those built by Trumpington. Its vaulting is pitched higher than that of the two eleventh-century bays and lower than the vaulting of the two bays to the east. At the east end of this bay on the south may be seen the springers from Trumpington's demolished vaulting. The late fifteenth-century doorway in the south wall led to a small room outside the main building and since destroyed. The two easternmost bays belong to the late thirteenth-century rebuilding. The detail of the wall arcading, of which only a fragment at the east end remains, is noticeably richer than that in the north aisle and is similar to that in the south aisle of the ambulatory. The destruction of the arcade in the easternmost bay

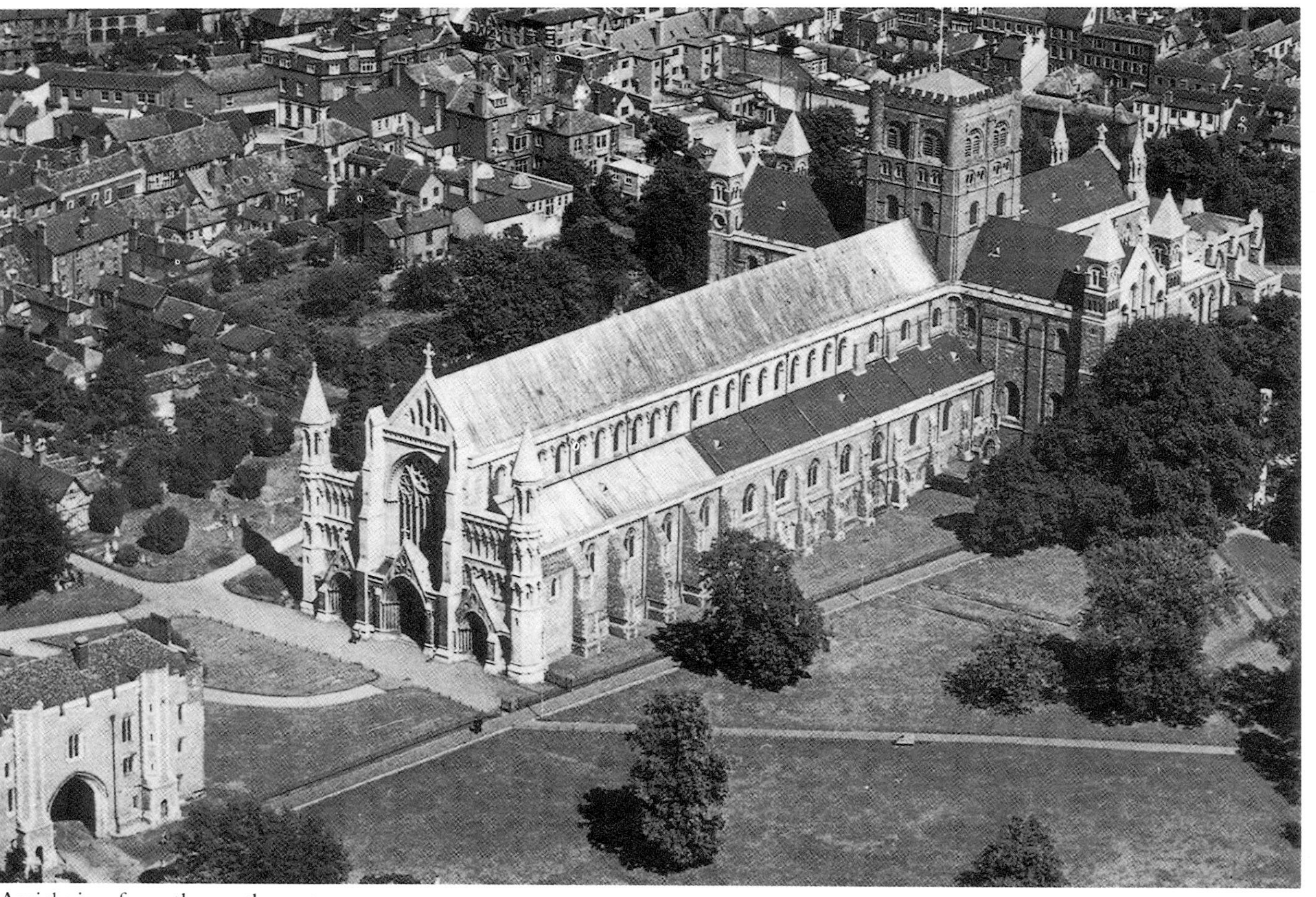

Aerial view from the south west

PLATE 2

Interior of Lady Chapel, looking east

Early 14th century

PLATE 3

Abbot Ramryge's Chantry Chapel c. 1521

The Watching Chamber Early 15th century

Central Tower, exterior from south west — Late 11th century

Duke Humphrey's Chantry Chapel 1441–7

Painted Crucifixion on pier of north arcade of Nave — Late 13th century

Lady Chapel, detail of window-splay

St. Alban's Shrine

Duke Humphrey's Chantry Chapel, details of frieze

1441–7

North side of Nave 13th and 11th centuries

Choir Screen

Late 14th century

Crossing from the north — Late 11th century

North arcade of Nave — Late 11th century

Roof of Nave   Late 15th century

Roof of Presbytery   Late 13th century

Triforium of South Transept | Late 11th century

Triforium of Nave, south side | 14th and 13th centuries

was due to the building in 1429 by Wheathampstead of a chapel to contain his tomb. One of the arcading shafts can still be seen at the east end of the bay. To the west of Wheathampstead's chapel was another chapel of late fifteenth-century date. It was separated from the aisle by the stone screen in the second bay from the east, now partly covered by a modern imitation of the original wall arcading. When first uncovered in the mid nineteenth century the screen had remains of decoration which included the Tudor Rose. If the decoration was contemporary with the construction the screen dates from very late in the fifteenth century and was probably the last alteration to the fabric before the Reformation.

The panel on the north wall of the westernmost bay is from the old ceiling of the north transept and represents the martyrdom of St. Alban.

The *Fittings* in the presbytery: The presbytery, because it contained the high altar and the shrine of St. Alban, was the holiest part of the church and it is here that all the later sepulchral monuments are concentrated. The object of devotion was the shrine of St. Alban which stood where its reconstructed pedestal now stands. This pedestal (Frontispiece), almost entirely of Purbeck marble with the exception of the canopy roofs which are of the soft stone called clunch, was found in pieces in 1872 in the wall which then blocked the east end of the presbytery. It is covered with foliage carving and with scenes from St. Alban's life. At the west end is shown his martyrdom (Plate 7) and at the east end the scourging that preceded it. On the south side are the figures of Offa of Mercia and, possibly, of St. Oswyn. In the niches the remains of decoration at one time included the leopards of England and the lilies of France. An entry in the 'Gesta Abbatum' records that Abbot John de Maryns (1302–8) removed and adorned the shrine and 'tumba' of St. Alban, and the existing work can probably be dated to this period. Of the shrine itself nothing remains and Thomas Baskerville, who visited St. Albans in 1681, recorded a tradition that it had been taken to France.

Second only in importance to the shrine of St. Alban was that of St. Amphibalus, the Christian who converted him, which stood in the centre of the westernmost bay of the ambulatory. The pedestal of the shrine was found in pieces in 1872 and is now in the north presbytery aisle. The initials R.W. on the north and south faces make it reasonably certain that this is the 'tumba' that was decorated at the cost of Ralph Whytchurche, the Sacrist, during the abbacy of Thomas Delamare (1349–96). At the west end the letters AMPHIB. . .S of the saint's name are legible.

As the fame and influence of Alban and Amphibalus spread, gifts to the shrine increased and it became necessary to maintain a constant guard over its treasures. For this purpose the wooden feretory loft or watching chamber (Plate 3) was built, on the north side of the presbytery opposite the shrine.

The lower storey has cupboards for holding relics and the slit in one of the cupboard doors may have been for coins to be slipped through. The upper chamber was for the monk on guard over the shrine. The beam dividing the two storeys has a series of carvings representing the Months and, perhaps, scenes from local life. The central carving on each side shows the Martyrdom of St. Alban. An entry in the St. Albans' *Book of Benefactors* seems to show that the chamber was set up in the early years of the fifteenth century. It is possible that the seated hart on the north side is meant for the badge of Richard II and that the chamber is therefore to be dated before 1399. But it is not very likely, for Richard was no favourite with the community at St. Albans, who suspected him of favouring Westminster at their expense. Their contemporary chronicler, Thomas of Walsingham, rarely misses an opportunity to tell stories to Richard's discredit. The countersunk hinge-ends of the cupboard doors are designed in an architectural manner and are of the early fifteenth century. In the cupboard is a small fragment of an ironwork screen of twelfth or thirteenth-century date.

Institutions are often beginning to decay when they seem at their greatest glory, and it is possible that the importance of St. Alban's shrine was declining in the fifteenth century. In any case, the fashion of the late middle ages demanded that high altar (Plate 13) and shrine be separated here as at Canterbury and Winchester; and so the reredos to the altar came to dominate this part of the church. There was probably always a low screen between the presbytery and the feretory, but until the erection of the present reredos the view eastwards from the central crossing must have been dominated by the most important feature—the high altar with the Saint's shrine towering above it. The reredos was built during the abbacy of William of Wallingford at the cost of 1,100 marks (£733 6s. 8d.) and is explicitly stated to have been completed in 1484, but a contribution of 100s. to its cost is recorded in 1487 and it was possibly not completed until then. The reredos is built of clunch and has suffered severely from ill-usage in the past. In the mid eighteenth century the central panels were filled with incongruous cherubs' heads. It was greatly restored at the end of the last century and all the statues and the cresting and canopies are new. It is closely comparable, both in date and design, with the great reredos at Winchester.

In the later middle ages funeral monuments became increasingly elaborate. The first step in this direction is shown by the funeral brass of Abbot Delamare, now in the chapel on the south side of the presbytery. This brass is one of the finest in England and is almost certainly the work of a Flemish artist working in this country. It was probably made between 1360 and 1370 and represents the abbot in his Mass vestments and wearing all the insignia of his position as a 'mitred Abbot'—the mitre, the shoes and the glove with a ring upon it. In the canopied niches are God the Father at the top, flanked by SS. Peter and Paul with other saints below, of which the first is St. Alban. The inscription fillet has the symbols of the four Evangelists in the corners and the abbot's arms—*Argent on a bend azure three eagles or*. The customary initial cross before the inscription is, somewhat unusually, placed saltire-wise and may be meant as a reference to the Abbey's arms—*Azure a saltire or*.

As an example of the growing fashion of erecting tombs and chantry chapels of increasing richness the monument of Humphrey of Gloucester, placed as near as possible to the Saint's shrine, is outstanding. Humphrey, whose chauvinist attitude to the disastrous French wars won him the ludicrous title of 'Good Duke Humphrey', was a friend of John of Wheathampstead and obtained in 1441 a licence to endow a chantry in St. Albans Church. He was killed in 1447 and the chantry was probably completed by then. The open lower stage was designed to take the tomb but Humphrey was, in fact, buried in the vault under the pavement and it is doubtful if the tomb was ever made. On the north side along the cornice are four shields of the duke's arms—France and England quarterly in a silver border. The niches were probably once filled with figures similar to those on the south. These are curiously foreshortened and squat figures and may well be of a different date from the structure. The whole surface of the stonework is panelled and carved with a device generally said to be 'daisies in a standing cup' and assumed to be Humphrey's badge. Sir Thomas Kendrick has suggested that they are, in fact, 'Gardens of Adonis'—a classical *memento mori* revived by some of the Humanists, of whom Humphrey was the most famous English patron of his time. If Sir Thomas is right this tomb must be amongst the earliest examples of Humanist influence on English church monuments (Plates 5 and 7).

Affixed to the south side of the monument is a lattice grille of wrought iron, with quatrefoil cresting along the top. This is probably of the third quarter of the fifteenth century. It is similar to the grille in Henry V's chapel at Westminster Abbey and may be by the same artist, Johnson. Although somewhat more sophisticated than the Westminster example, the grille retains traces of woodworking technique.

To the west of Humphrey's monument is the chantry chapel generally called that of Abbot Wheathampstead. The evidence points rather to its having been erected by Abbot William of Wallingford for his own tomb and it has, in quatrefoil panel above the cornice, the rayed rose badge of Edward IV. The work is noticeably coarser than that on Duke Humphrey's chantry chapel. The iron grille is probably contemporary.

The latest of the chantry chapels, on the north side of the presbytery, and opposite Wallingford's, is that of Abbot Ramryge who died in 1521. The chapel (Plate 3) is built of clunch, is in two stages, and has a delicate fan-vaulted roof. The panelling is enriched with the abbot's rebus—a ram with a collar and the letters RYGE. The cornice has the arms of Henry VIII. Chantry chapels built in two stages are not common and it is possible that the upper stage was used to accommodate the singers. On the floor is an incised slab with the figure of the abbot. In the seventeenth century the chapel was appropriated by a local family, the Faringdons, who have dignified it with their arms.

Although the chapels are the most conspicuous of the existing funeral monuments, the Abbey has a collection of brasses, probably unique in variety and range, that well illustrate the development of brass work in England from the early fourteenth to the early seventeenth century. It is noteworthy that the brasses, or the slabs for the brasses, of nearly all the abbots from the early fourteenth to the mid-fifteenth century can be identified. The earliest is that of Abbot John de Berkhampstead, 1291–1302, in the presbytery a few paces west of the altar steps. The brass has gone but part of the marginal inscription in Norman French remains. '[Abbot John lies] here May God have mercy on his soul you who pass by say a pater and an ave for his soul. All. . .' Of the brasses of the other abbots only that of Delamare remains at all complete.

By the middle of the fifteenth century the more expensive practice of building chantry chapels for the abbots was becoming usual, but brasses were becoming commoner for minor officials of the monastery. The earliest example of these is the slab in the north transept, probably of Brother William Stubbarde, who had charge of much of the Abbey's building work at the end of the fourteenth century. The latest is the slab in the south transept—the brass from which is now on a board in the vestry—of Thomas Rutland, sub-prior, who died in 1521. The best preserved is that of Robert Beauver, just to the north of Abbot Berkhampstead's slab. It is probably of about 1460 and portrays a Benedictine monk in gown and cowl holding in his hands, uplifted in prayer, a bleeding heart on which are six drops of blood. A scroll on the left side of the head has the words 'Cor mundum in me crea Deus' (Make in me a clean heart, O God), and below the figure is a Latin inscription—'Here lies Brother Robert Beauver, formerly monk of this monastery, who continuously for 46 years and more served the convent of the monastery in various offices, great and small; that is, in the offices of third prior, kitchener, refectorer and infirmarer and in the offices of sub-refectorer and spicerar of this convent. For whose soul, O most Dear Brothers, vouchsafe to pour forth prayers to the most High Judge, the Most Pious Lord, Jesus Christ, that He may grant to him pardon of his sins.'

Brasses of the laity do not occur at St. Albans before the fifteenth century and, until the Reformation, seem to be mostly of men who had served or helped the Abbey. The earliest is that of Thomas Fayrman and his wife, in the north aisle of the presbytery. Fayrman, who died in 1411, had been bailiff of St. Albans and burial in the Abbey was probably a mark of gratitude for good service. In the presbytery, to the south of Abbot Berkhampstead's slab, is the slab of Bartholomew Halley and Florence his wife; the brass is on the board in the vestry. Halley died in 1468 and he and his wife are dressed in the costume of the period. Below the brass is an inscription in English—it appears always to have been upside-down—'Here lyeth Bartholomew Halley and Florens his wife. [Of your] charite sey for these tweyn soules a paternoster and [an ave].' Halley too had served the Abbey and in 1465 had won an important lawsuit for the abbot. One of the best-preserved brasses is that, on the south side of the presbytery, of Sir Anthony Grey who died in 1480. He is portrayed in the extravagant armour of the period, with the Yorkist badges of suns and roses on a collar round his neck. At the corners of the slab are four indents for shields; one of the shields is on the board in the vestry. After the Reformation, when the Abbey was the parish church, brasses of the laity became commoner and one of the best is that of Ralph Rowlatt, merchant of the Staple at Calais, in the south aisle of the presbytery. Rowlatt died in 1543 and the brass, which has the space for the day and year of his death left blank, was probably made before that date. Below the figures of Rowlatt and his wife are the indent for the figures of three sons and the brass of six daughters. This is a common feature on brasses but is not found on any other brass at St. Albans. The latest brass of all is dated 1604. It is merely an inscription, to Agnes Skelton, and is now on the board in the vestry.

By the early seventeenth century brasses were going out of fashion and, for those who could afford it, sculptured tombs or wall monuments were generally provided. The painting on the north wall of the south aisle of Ralph Maynard, who died in 1613, appears to be a less expensive imitation of this practice. The dead man is portrayed in contemporary costume in a kneeling position, in the manner common on tombs of the period: although the medium is painting and not sculpture the similarity of composition is obvious.

THE CENTRAL CROSSING (Plates 4 and 10)

The central crossing with its tower is perhaps the only one belonging to the greater eleventh-century churches which still survives. It was probably originally covered by a low pyramidal roof. William of Trumpington in the middle of the thirteenth century added an octagonal lead-covered wooden spire. This was later replaced by a low 'Hertfordshire Spike', possibly at the end of the fifteenth or beginning of the sixteenth century. The tower stands on four slightly stilted semi-circular arches. In the third stage is a gallery in the thickness of the wall. In the topmost storey between each pair of windows is a painted coat of arms, of Edward I, of his wife, his brother and his uncle. On the east are Edward's arms—*gules three leopards or* (England); on the west those of his wife, Eleanor of Castile—*gules a castle or* (Castile) quartering *argent a lion purple* (Leon). On the south are the arms of his brother Edmund of Lancaster—England with *a label of five points azure;* and on the north are the arms of his uncle Richard, Earl of Cornwall and King of the Romans, *argent a lion gules crowned or in a border sable bezanty*. The rood beam which originally crossed the eastern arch has disappeared except for one small fragment projecting from the north face of the south-east pier and another which it is hoped will be on exhibition in the Treasury. The tower was saved from falling and made safe in 1872, when a great pit with charred timbers in it was found under the north-east pier. This is probably evidence of an attempt, possibly by the same Sir Richard Lee who destroyed the monastic buildings, to undermine the tower and with it the whole church in order to use or sell the ruins as building materials. The battlements were rebuilt by Lord Grimthorpe and the string-course was renewed in Chilmark stone. The plaster which had covered the tower was removed and the red brick exposed to view.

THE NORTH TRANSEPT

The north transept is, with the exception of the north wall, much as Paul of Caen built it. It is interesting to observe that there are close resemblances between the north and south transepts at St. Albans and those of the Abbey Church of St. Stephen at Caen. The original apsidal chapels on the east side were probably removed early in the fifteenth century. The blocked entrances into their upper storeys can be seen. Fifteenth-century windows were inserted into the blocked ground-floor entrances but these were removed by Lord Grimthorpe who put in the present lancets. Grimthorpe also removed William of Wallingford's great fifteenth-century north window and put in the present window. In the triforium on the east are two re-used Saxon baluster shafts. They were not long enough for their present position and have had extra capitals and bases added to them. That there are only two such shafts in the north transept and six in the south is probably an indication that the north transept was built later, when the supply was running short. The pilaster buttresses have been cut away at the base, possibly to make room for altars beneath them. The present ceiling is by Lord Grimthorpe and replaces a painted ceiling. It has been raised above the original ceiling level, which was probably on the tops of the buttresses. The painting on the buttress on the east was discovered beneath the plaster in 1845. The subject is the rather unusual one of 'The Incredulity of St. Thomas' and it is probably of the late fifteenth century. The red background appears to be powdered with Crowns of Thorns. In the south window on the east are four shields, possibly from Abbot Delamare's glazing of the cloisters, of the arms of Edward III, Old France and England quarterly, and of three of his sons: of Edward, Prince of Wales, Old France and England quarterly with a silver label; of Lionel, Duke of Clarence, Old France and England quarterly having a silver label with a canton gules on each point; and of John of Gaunt, Old France and England quarterly with an ermine label. In the seventeenth century a wooden gallery for the scholars of the school in the Lady chapel stood across the south end of the transept. It seems to have been removed early in the nineteenth century.

THE SOUTH TRANSEPT (Plate 12)

Although the south transept is roughly contemporary with the north there is, apart from the evidence mentioned before, some indication that it is rather earlier than the north and a suggestion that a change of design occurred soon after the south transept was begun. In the south jamb of the south clearstorey window of the west wall there is a stone shaft with a cushion capital. This is a feature not found elsewhere in the church, although it may have occurred in the destroyed presbytery clearstorey, and may mean that a richer design than that carried out was at first intended, and that the Norman church was not, in fact, completed in a single building campaign. The transept has undergone no great structural reconstruction but many alterations have been made in it. The first of these was the replacement in the early thirteenth century of two of the original windows of the ground stage on the west by the present lancets. These had the effect of displacing the central shafts in each bay of the triforium, and the present rectangular pillars with roll mouldings at the angles and plain leaves on the capitals are of this date. These alterations were probably made to give more light to the assemblage of figures placed in the transept together with the new image of the Virgin (described as the 'elegantissimam' and 'nobilem Mariolam') elaborately carved by Walter of Colchester. The original apsidal chapels on the east were probably removed early in the fourteenth century. The northern had been used as a Lady chapel and with the completion of the present Lady chapel had no further purpose.

The chapels were replaced by vestries and the present doorways of fourteenth-century design were inserted. A treasury was built over the northern vestry and it is possible that the now blocked chamber at the north end of the west wall of the transept with its two-light fifteenth-century window was built to accommodate a monk keeping watch over the entrance to the treasury. The vaulted eleventh-century opening was the original entrance into the transept from the cloisters. The internal arch has been restored.

The south wall of the transept has undergone the greatest alterations. The original windows were removed and a great window was inserted by William of Wallingford some time before 1484. This was blown down in the famous storm that swept all of southern England in 1703, and was roughly replaced by a wooden window. This again, with the whole of the south wall, was removed by Lord Grimthorpe and the wall rebuilt and the present lancets inserted. The doorway in the wall originally opened into a barrel-vaulted passage, between the transept and the chapter house, leading from the cloister to the monks' cemetery. The passage was destroyed by Grimthorpe but its twelfth-century west doorway was inserted here. The outer orders of the doorway are original but the inner one is modern and, under Grimthorpe's direction, was carved with great care and fidelity to the original in the hope of confusing and confounding some of his many antiquarian critics.

THE NAVE (Plates 8 and 12)

The nave, now of thirteen bays, was originally of ten and of these nine remain on the north and three on the south. The piers of the arcade are extremely solid, even for the eleventh century. Their plain appearance and the absence of mouldings on them is partly to be explained by the hardness of the Roman brick from Verulamium, of which they are composed, which made carving almost impossible. There is a difference in section between the bays east of the choir screen and those to the west of it, and the design of the painted decoration on the underneath of the arches changes at the same point. This may, again, be an indication of a break in the progress of the building under Paul of Caen. In the fifteenth century the roofs of the aisles were repaired and their pitch lowered. This meant that the gallery was now open to the sky and had, in fact, become a lower clearstorey. The present windows were then inserted in the old openings and were presumably glazed. When Lord Grimthorpe re-raised the aisle roofs at the end of the last century the gallery reverted to its original function. The imposts of the old triforium openings and an indication of the outer order of the arch may be seen on the north. In the gallery, on each side of the present openings, is a blank traceried panel. It is clear that the old openings were partly filled in when the fifteenth-century windows were inserted. The design of the original openings is difficult to determine. It is possible that they were similar to the two-light windows under a relieving arch in the central tower, but there are no certain indications of this to be seen today. In the third bay from the east windows were not inserted in the fifteenth century. It was here that the pulpitum stood and prevented any internal alterations. The openings were however blocked externally, presumably when the triforium was opened to the sky.

The four westernmost bays on the north and five on the south, together with some mutilated fragments of the west front are from the westward extension of John de Cella and William of Trumpington. Although almost all of the west front was rebuilt by Lord Grimthorpe, there are still bits of original arcading to be seen behind his work in the north porch. These are sufficiently similar to some of the details of St. Hugh's Choir at Lincoln, 1192–9, for the two works to be more or less contemporary. The facade was designed to have flanking towers and was altogether richer than the nave bays. There is evidence that a stone vault was planned for the nave, but like the towers, never actually built. The vault-shafts at triforium level imply a sexpartite vault over each bay as in the transepts at Lincoln. The abandoment of the vaulting left the flat faces of the piers between the windows exposed to view, and these were covered with a simplified design of shallow sinkings.

The differences and changes provide a basis for distinguishing between early and late phases; but even so it is not possible to say with certainty which is the work of John or William. However, the western respond of the westernmost bay of the south arcade is richer than any of those to the east, while the easternmost bay of that arcade is without any signs of preparation for vaulting. It is therefore likely that the new west front was erected while the old was still standing, that building proceeded from west to east and that the decision to dispense with a stone vault was taken only when the easternmost bay was being built.

Across the north aisle at the fourth pier from the west and across the south aisle at the fifth pier are quadrant arches. There is no indication in the eleventh-century bays of any attempt at vaulting and the abutments on the aisle side of the arcade piers on the north show that there were quadrant arches throughout the north aisle. The south aisle was probably similar. The taking down of an extra bay on the south is perhaps an indication that the south arcade was already showing signs of the weakness that led to the fall of the next five bays to the east in 1323.

The repair of these bays was begun by Abbot Hugh of Eversden but lingered under his successor Richard of Wallingford and was not completed until the abbacy of Michael of Mentmore (1335–49). Although this rebuilding can be easily recognised by its richer and more developed features—the ball-flower enrichment of the orders of the triforium arches and the trefoiled tracery in the spandrels—an attempt was made to harmonise it with the thirteenth-century work to the west and in consequence the triforium has more, and the clearstorey less, importance than is usual in work of this date. The stops of the labels of the arcade arches are carved with human heads, generally supposed to represent Abbot Hugh of Eversden, Isabel of France, her husband Edward II and Master Henry Wy, 'Master of the

Works' at the Abbey. Edward II died in 1327 and it is possible that the arcade had been completed by then. The shields under the string-course at the base of the triforium have the leopards of England alternating with the cross and martlets of Edward the Confessor, the three crowns either of St. Oswyn or Mercia and the lilies of France.

Choir Screen (Plate 9). It seems likely, from contemporary accounts, that the collapse of the south arcade in 1323 either destroyed or severely damaged the then existing rood screen. Once the repair of the fabric had been completed, the replacement of the screen was essential. In the greater Benedictine churches it appears to have been usual to bring the choir screen forward several bays into the nave but today St. Albans is the only one that possesses, *in situ*, this satisfactory westward termination. The present screen is built of clunch and was probably completed some time before 1380. The difference in design at the north and south ends is probably due to the irregularity between the north and south piers of the arcade. The present continuation of the screen across the north aisle is a modern addition by Lord Grimthorpe. The tracery in the heads of the doors is worth comparing with that in the upper storey of the watching chamber of perhaps thirty years later. One bay to the east of the screen stood the pulpitum erected by Walter of Colchester in the thirteenth century. During the restorations of 1875–6 the foundations of the choir stalls were found, extending from the east side of the crossing to the site of the pulpitum and leaving a small ante-choir between there and the screen. The choir stalls were probably of the early fourteenth century for in 1315 Edward II gave 100 marks and a quantity of timber to the Abbey for the choir. On the south-west face of the pier on the north side can be seen the remains of the steps of a staircase to the loft above the pulpitum.

Wall and Ceiling Paintings. Decorations on the arches of the piers of the north arcade and elsewhere formed part of a general decorative scheme that included the nave, the crossing and the transepts and was probably executed about 1220. The voussoirs of the arches, for example the tower arches, are painted in alternating colours and on the soffits of the arches and some of the piers is a plain masonry pattern, chevrons and lozenges. In the north arcade of the nave the masonry pattern is elaborated with roses and stars and appears to be somewhat later than the rest.

The paintings on the west faces of the piers of the north arcade form a remarkable double series of the Crucifixion in the upper panels, and of the Virgin Mary in the lower panels (Plates 6 and 10); starting from the west, they illustrate the development of English art throughout the thirteenth century. Those on the first pier are very similar in style to the painted ceiling of Peterborough Cathedral and were probably painted about 1215. On the next pier, in the Crucifixion, the legs of Christ are more contorted and are fastened over each other with a single nail; this painting probably belongs to the second quarter of the century. On the third and fourth piers the subjects are framed within an arcade, with capitals very similar to those of William of Trumpington's work in the nave, and were probably painted between 1250 and 1260. The fifth pier has a Crucifixion of the fully developed type of the end of the century, with the figure of Christ contorted in a double curve. The curious blackness of the faces, hands and feet of the figures is probably due to the use of veneda, a black pigment frequently used in thirteenth-century work as an under-painting for flesh colours, which has remained after the flesh colours have worn off. The paintings on the south faces of the piers—SS. Christopher, Thomas of Canterbury, Osyth and probably Edward the Confessor and the pilgrim—are possibly of varying dates. In the last two paintings the figures stand on pedestals and are, in this respect, similar to the late thirteenth-century figure of St. Faith at Westminster. The figure of St. Thomas of Canterbury may be the image that Robert de Trench had painted about 1380. All the paintings were white-washed over in the later middle ages and only rediscovered in the nineteenth century. These paintings were not the work of rustic craftsmen but of men who were among the most competent artists of their time and who helped to give St. Albans its reputation.

There are remains of paintings between the clearstorey windows at the east end of the nave. They are badly faded, but appear to have formed part of a series representing the Apostles. One has been identified as St. John and one as St. James. They were probably painted in the second quarter of the thirteenth century.

Probably the last piece of decoration to be carried out in the nave before the Dissolution was the painting of the ceiling (Plate 11). The western part is modern but the ceiling above the choir is probably of the mid fifteenth century and is remarkable for its display of heraldry. The main purpose of its thirty-two panels appears to be to glorify the House of Lancaster, and for this reason the arms of foreign kings connected with that House by marriage, such as the kings of Aragon and Portugal, are introduced. The central panel shows the Coronation of the Virgin. The shields alternate with panels bearing the sacred monogram I.H.S.

On a pillar of the north arcade is an inscription to Sir John de Mandeville, the fourteenth-century 'Traveller'. Sir John de Mandeville, or whoever the romancer may have been who used that pen-name, claimed to have been born at St. Albans and later tradition rounded off the story by burying him there as well. In fact, he was certainly buried at Liège and was probably not born at St. Albans. A traveller who visited the Abbey in 1681 recorded a couplet 'in the roof of the church, over his body' which deserves not to be lost:

'Lo in this Inn of travel doth Lye
One rich in nothing but a memory'.

THE NORTH AISLE

The north aisle mainly corresponds in date with the adjoining portions of the nave. The eastern end of the aisle has been turned into a vestry by Lord Grimthorpe. Above the entry into the vestry from the north transept are the carved figures of a Lion and Unicorn, from the old Mayoral pew; the west end is enclosed by the continuation of the choir screen across the aisle. The east and south sides are enclosed by seventeenth-century panelling removed from the chancel. Some of this was apparently set up in 1692–3 and is the work of a local carver. The six bays immediately west of the choir screen are of the eleventh century, but some of the windows were later encased in stone by William of Trumpington.

In the four westernmost bays the north wall is modern. There was formerly an arcade here between the aisle and the chapel of St. Andrew, a parochial chapel set aside for the use of the parishioners. The first chapel of St. Andrew was dedicated some time before 1115 and the door in the fifth bay from the west probably opened into it. It was pulled down at the beginning of the thirteenth century, when the nave was extended westwards, and was rebuilt level with the new west front. The bases of the two easternmost piers of the arcade were found in the 1870s in the north wall of the aisle and corresponded with the bases of the western nave piers. The chapel was again rebuilt in 1454–62 but the arcade between the chapel and the nave was probably not altered. After the Dissolution, when the Abbey itself became the parish church, the chapel was no longer needed and was pulled down. The arcade was then blocked to form an exterior wall.

The door now propped against the wall of the west end of the aisle and its companion in the south aisle are probably of the fifteenth century and may have been the doors of the north and south porches.

THE SOUTH AISLE

The south side is of the same date as the corresponding bays of the nave, but its vaulting, with the exception of the five bays built after 1323, is modern. In the south wall of the westernmost bay is the blocked arch into the projected, but never completed, south-west tower.

The windows in the first three bays from the west are modern insertions in the former blank wall against which the abbot's lodging abutted. The fourteenth-century windows in the sixth to tenth bays came down low internally but the glass was kept high; above the roof-level of the north walk of the cloister. In the seventh bay was a small door into the cloister and a passage in the thickness of the wall led into the abbot's chapel above the abbot's lodging. In the second bay from the east is a thirteenth-century tomb recess with a sixteenth-century inscription above it to the hermits

Roger and Sigar. The memory of Sigar's saintliness was cherished at St. Albans. He was so devout that even the singing of the nightingales disturbed his meditations in his cell at Northaw. He prayed to God to abate the nuisance, and from that day no nightingale has sung in Northaw Wood. In the easternmost bay is a late fourteenth-century doorway with a modern exterior into the cloister. The carved and painted shields in the spandrels have the arms of Richard II (Old France, *azure powdered with fleurs-de-lis or*, quartering England, *gules three leopards or*) and of the Abbey (*azure a saltire or*). The latter appears to be the earliest known representation of these arms, with the possible exception of the initial cross, placed saltire-wise, of the inscription on Abbot Delamare's brass. In any case it seems probable that these arms originated during the reign of that aristocratic and well-connected abbot.

Graffiti. In the northern entry of the west porch, scratched on the stonework of the south wall, is a representation of an eagle. The bird is drawn with its head turned back and with an exaggerated curved beak. The stonework below it has been very much mutilated and no evidence remains of the original architectural setting. It is possible that the scratching was done shortly after the completion of the porch in the early thirteenth century, but it may be noted that the eagle was one of the favourite motifs of Abbot John of Wheathampstead and appears, with the lamb, in his decoration of the presbytery vault.

In the plaster on the wall of the north aisle, opposite the seventh bay of the nave-arcade, is a scratching of a wheel. It is eight feet in diameter with a pierced hub and with six broad spokes, four and a half inches across; between the heads of the spokes, there is a semi-circular cusping and there is cusped decoration within the rim which, on the western side, straggles outside the perimeter of the wheel. The whole upper part of the wheel and the lower part of the rim have been mutilated but enough remains to suggest a design for a wheel-window. The manner of the design suggests the twelfth century. It is almost exactly reproduced in the heads of the side lights of the west window put in by Lord Grimthorpe.

MONASTIC BUILDINGS

With a community of about eighty monks entertaining and negotiating with kings and playing an important part in the country's history, the Abbey needed a great number of buildings of various kinds. Besides those for the use and accommodation of the monks, the cloister, dormitory, refectory, chapter house and others, the Abbey had several buildings for lodging important guests and their retinues. There was a special chamber—the Aula Regia or Royal Hall—for the visits of the king and, at one time, stabling for two hundred horses. Activity in the building, rebuilding and altering of all the various structures was almost uninterrupted. With the exception of the Great Gatehouse and part of the 'Waxhouse Gate', which still stand, and the 'River Gate' , which was demolished in 1722, most of these buildings were pulled down soon after the Dissolution. Their general position is indicated by the grass-covered banks and mounds stretching down the slope to the south of the church. From documents and excavations it is, however, possible to determine the site of many specific buildings.

At St. Albans the usual practice was followed of placing the monastic buildings to the south of the church. The great cloister had its north and east walls formed by the south wall of the nave and the west wall of the south transept. The fall of five bays of the nave in 1323 destroyed the north walk of the cloister and the rebuilding was begun by Richard of Wallingford. The cloister was the general 'work-room' of the monastery, and Wallingford, who seems to have been a practically-minded man, appears to have set about its rebuilding with an energy that was in great contrast to his indifference to the church. The tracery of the arcading of the rebuilt cloister, although much later than that of the windows of the Lady chapel, shows no advance upon it. Immediately south of the great cloister was the refectory or frater which was rebuilt about 1388. Excavation in 1924 found its north and south walls.

The chapter house lay to the south of the south transept, separated from it by the slype, the passage between the cloister and the monks' cemetery. The excavations which took place in 1920 and 1937 revealed the site of the building and those of 1978 have elucidated its history. The earliest chapter house, built by Abbot Paul between 1077 and 1088 over part of an Anglo-Saxon cemetery, had an apsidal east end and was about 50 feet long, including the apse, and about 26 feet wide (Plate 14A). It was apparently a very plain building and inadequate for the size of the community and before the middle of the twelfth century it had been extended, again with an apse, to a length of about 70 feet (Plate 14B). At some time between 1154 and 1166 Abbot Robert of Gorham pulled down Paul's building and its extension and built a new chapter house on the same site, 29 feet wide, 91 feet long and without an apse (Plate 14C). It had a tiled floor and was richly decorated internally and, at least towards the cloister, externally as well. The skeleton of this building stood until after the Dissolution but its appearance had been transformed in the late fifteenth century when a stone fan-vault was added and new windows cut and filled with Flemish stained glass.

The monks' dormitory, the dorter, lay immediately to the south of the chapter house. The excavations of 1978 have established that the whole of the dorter range was rebuilt some time before 1195, and that the undercroft of the dorter was reconstructed between then and 1214. A further reconstruction took place between 1396 and 1401 (Plate 14D).

The outer parlour of the abbot's house, with the abbot's chapel above, lay immediately south of the third and fourth bays from the west of the nave. The abbot's house seems to have been completed originally in the middle of the twelfth century, but was greatly added to in later times, especially by Abbots Delamare and Wheathampstead. It was probably in a room in the abbot's house, called in the fifteenth century the 'Clok Chambre', that Richard of Wallingford's great clock was kept.

South and slightly west of the west front were the 'Aula Regia' and the various guest chambers, and south-west of them the stables and the River Gate. The old infirmary, built in the early twelfth century, was possibly on the site of the present Orchard House, south of the presbytery. A new infirmary was built shortly before 1427 and there is some documentary evidence to suggest that it was near the Great Gateway and the site of the old almonry. A gate on the town side called the 'New Gate' or 'Waxhouse Gate' was built by Wheathampstead about 1427 and part of it, a plastered arch, still stands in the High Street. North of the north transept are the foundations of what may have been the sacristy.

The Great Gateway (Plate 1)

The Great Gateway, the only remaining monastic building, owes its survival to the decision of the town magistrates in 1553 to use it as a jail. It continued to be used for this purpose, and as a court house, until 1871 when the grammar school was moved here from the Lady chapel. The former gateway was blown down in a storm, probably that of 1362, and the new one was probably completed by 1365. A licence to crenellate had been obtained by Abbot Delamare in 1357 and the new gateway and a wall from the gateway to the Aula Regia—the latter built apparently under the general direction of Henry Yevele, the King's master mason—probably formed part of a general scheme of defence against the townspeople. The lower chambers of the new gateway were used as a jail. The townspeople apparently recognised the political implications of the abbot's building and in 1381, during the Peasants' Rising, threatened him with the destruction of his new gateway if he refused their demands.

The gatehouse is built mainly of flint rubble but with some Roman bricks and occasional blocks of stone. One of the chambers on the ground floor of the west side has vaulting made up of re-used thirteenth-century ribs and it seems likely that considerable material from the old gateway and the old almonry was re-used in the new building. The original roof was of lead and low-pitched; it was replaced in 1789 by the present high-pitched roof with tiles. In 1856 many of the old windows were restored. The parapet, which had probably been built of the soft Tottenhoe clunch, had to be reconstructed at the end of the fourteenth century. What the Abbey's chronicler called 'a hard Kentish stone', presumably Kentish rag, was used. An excavation, carried out about 1900, claimed to have shown that the ground course of the wall from the gateway to the Aula Regia and the ground course of the Great Gate were also of Kentish rag. This appears to be the only time when Kentish rag was used at St. Albans and its presence may perhaps be attributed to the advice of Henry Yevele, who had had considerable experience of the stone. The building of the Great Gate was carried out by the Brothers, William Stubard and John of Bokedene, who had control of much of the Abbey's building work at the time.

Printed in the United Kingdom for Her Majesty's Stationery Office
Dd 240089 C55 10/89 498 53309

Great Reredos c. 1485, restored

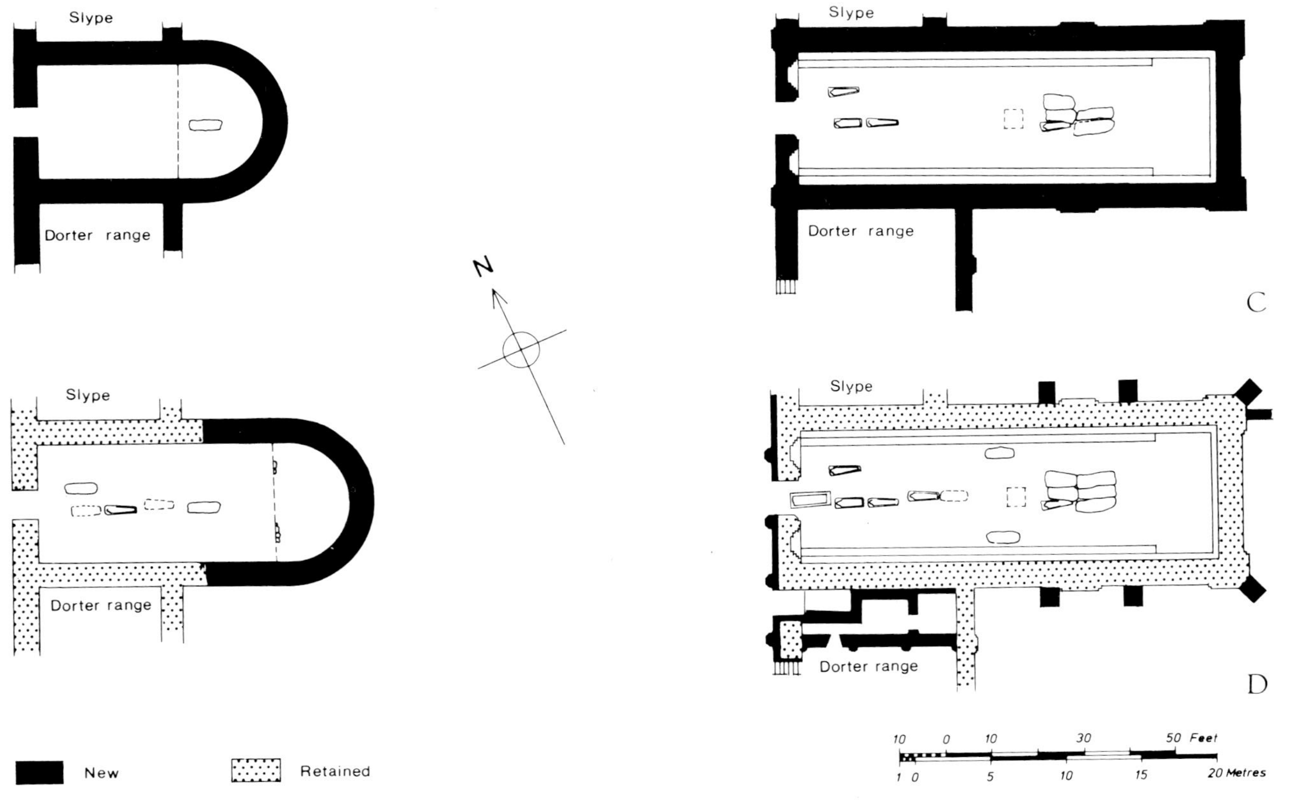

Chapter House. Interpretation of building sequence: A, 1077–88; B, between 1093 and 1151(?); C, between 1154 (1159?) and 1195; D, by 1539 (new work here represents various phases in building and reconstruction of both chapter house and dorter undercroft which took place between 1195 and the Dissolution). After drawings by M. Groves and B. Kjølbye-Biddle in 'The Medieval Chapter House of St. Albans Abbey, and its Excavation in 1978', *Expedition* 22, 1980, fig. 7.

SCALE OF FEET

10 20 30 40 50 60 70 80 90

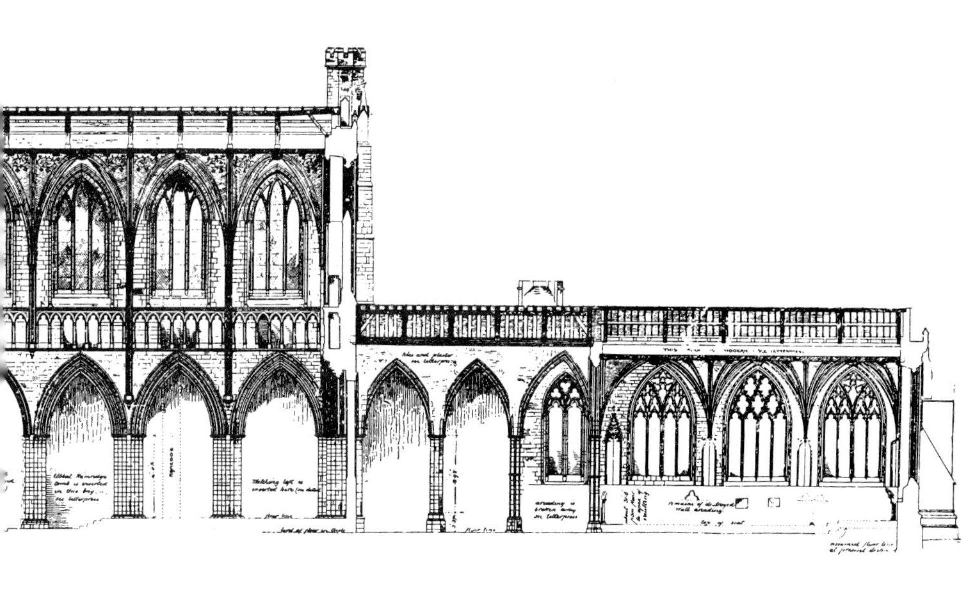

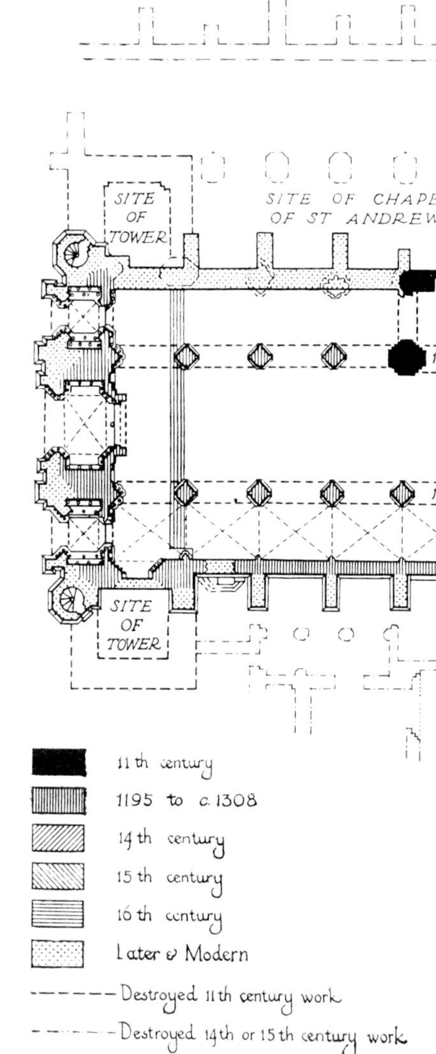
SITE
OF
TOWER
SITE OF CHAPEL
OF ST ANDREW
13
17
SITE
OF
TOWER
11 th century
1195 to c. 1308
14 th century
15 th century
16 th century
Later & Modern
Destroyed 11th century work
Destroyed 14th or 15th century work

ST. ALBAN

Scale of Feet
10 0 10 20 30 40 50 60 70 80 90 100
LAY CEMETERY
NORTH TRANSEPT
VESTRY
CHOIR
SITE OF PULPITUM
PRESBYTERY
SOUTH TRANSEPT
SITE OF CLOISTER
SITE OF CHAPTER HOUSE
SITE OF DORTER RANGE
F
G
B
A Watching Chambe
B Shrine and Altar
C Shrine of St. Amp
D Chapel of the Trar
E Chapel of Wheatl
F Chantry Chapel of
G Chantry Chapel
Abbot Wallingfo
H Chantry Chapel
Humphrey of Glou

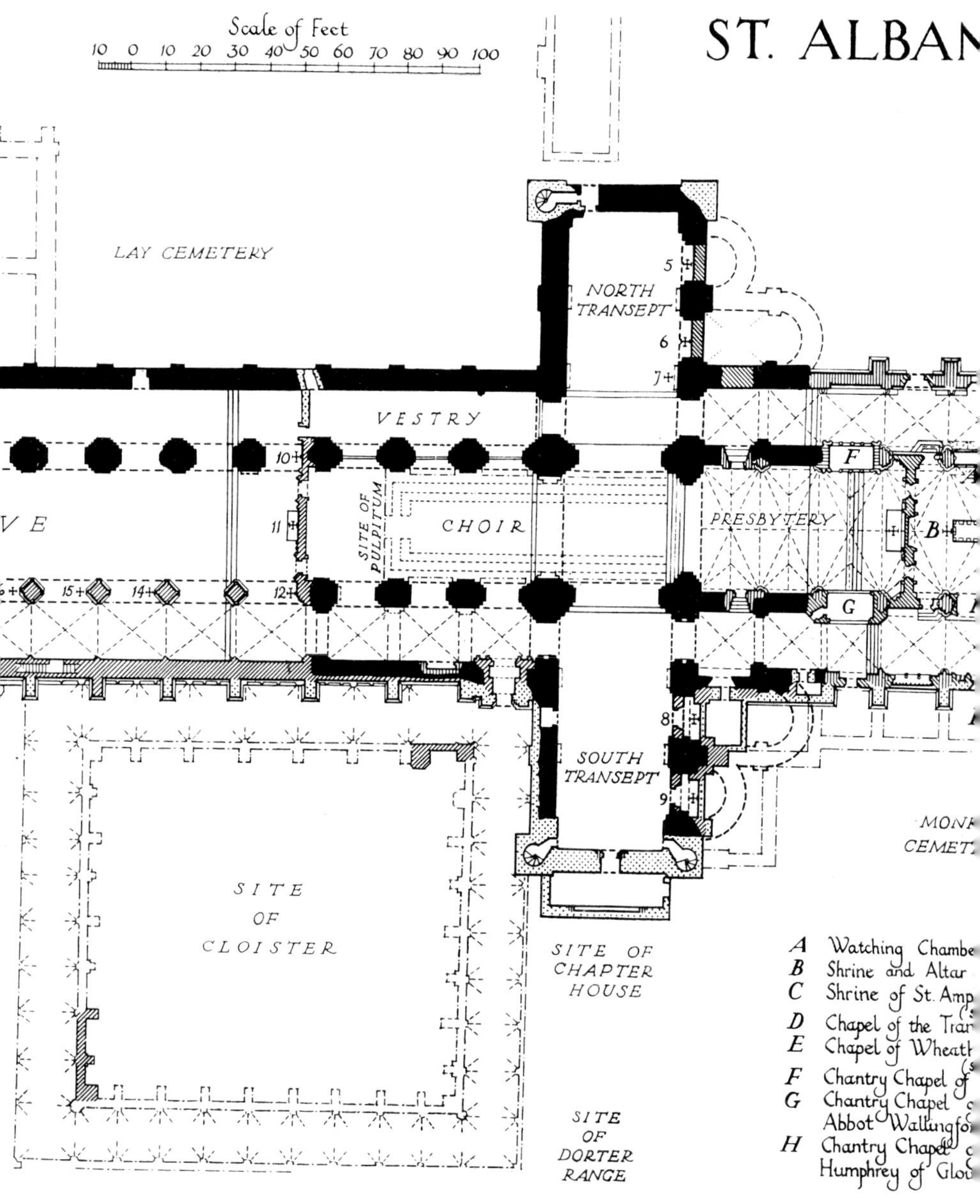

IS CATHEDRAL

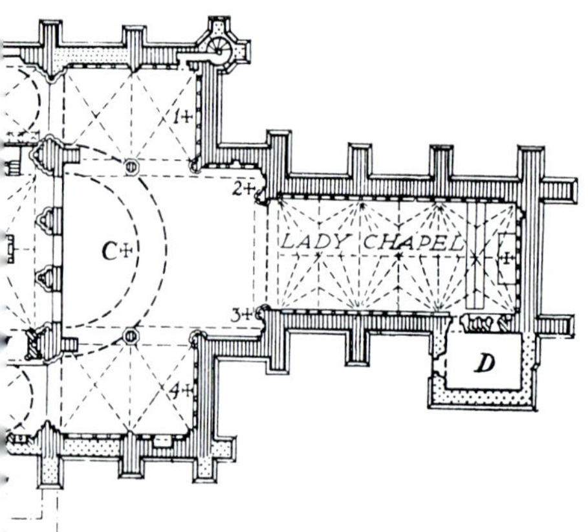

Sites of Altars :

1 St. Michael & St. Katherine
2 St. Edmund
3 St. Peter
4 Our Lady of the Four Tapers
5 Holy Trinity
6 St Citha
7 Bowing Rood
8 St. John the Evangelist
9 St. Stephen
10 St. Thomas of Canterbury
11 Our Lady
12 St. Benedict
13 St. Katherine
14 Our Lady
15 St. Benedict
16 St. Thomas of Canterbury
17 Our Lady at the Pillar

S'
RY
f St. Alban
balus
e of)
figuration
mpstead
te of)
Abbot Ramryge
ester